Fact Finders®

EXTREME LIFE

MEAT-EATING PLANTS AND OTHER EXTREME PLANT LIFE

BY JUNE PRESZLER

Consultant:
Jerry D. Davis
Honorary Fellow
Botany Department
University of Wisconsin, Madison

Capstone
press®

Mankato, Minnesota

Fact Finders are published by Capstone Press,
1710 Roe Crest Drive, North Mankato, Minnesota 56003.
www.capstonepub.com

022013
007180R

 Books published by Capstone Press are manufactured with paper
containing at least 10 percent post-consumer waste.

Library of Congress Cataloging-in-Publication Data
Preszler, June, 1954–
    Meat-eating plants and other extreme plant life / by June Preszler.
    p. cm. — (Fact finders. Extreme life)
    Summary: "Describes the world of plants, including characteristics, life cycles, and where they
live" — Provided by publisher.
    Includes bibliographical references and index.
    ISBN–13: 978–1–4296–1268–5 (hardcover)
    ISBN–10: 1–4296–1268–1 (hardcover)
    1. Carnivorous plants — Juvenile literature. 2. Plants — Juvenile literature. I. Title. II. Series.
QK917.P66 2008
580 — dc22   2007026966

Editorial Credits
Megan Schoeneberger and Lori Shores, editors; Alison Thiele, designer;
    Danielle Ceminsky, illustrator; Linda Clavel, photo researcher

Photo Credits
AnimalsAnimals/Earth Scenes/David M. Dennis, cover; OSF/G. I. Bernard, 14; P. Sharpe, 21
Corbis/Chinch Gryniewicz; Ecoscene, 17
Getty Images Inc./Adam Jones, 26
NASA, 28 (right)
NASA project/Texas A&M University/Ron Lacey/Fred Davies/Drs. Chuanjiu He, 28 (left)
Peter Arnold/BIOS Delobelle Jean-Philippe, 12; D. HEUCLIN, 11; PHONE/P. GOETGHELUCK, 5
Shutterstock/chai kian shin, 13; Denise Kappa, 23; Gordon Swanson, 27; Ilja Mašík, 9; Joe Gough,
    25; Jonny McCullagh, 7; Ke Wang, 19; Vova Pomortzeff, 15
Visuals Unlimited/John Gerlach, 20

TABLE OF CONTENTS

CHAPTER 1

THE PLANT KINGDOM

Imagine this. Along comes a hungry ant. The ant smells something sweet. It looks up and sees a flat leaf with a bright red spot. The ant thinks, "Lunch!"

The ant doesn't know it, but it is about to walk into a trap — a Venus flytrap, to be exact. The flytrap has little trigger hairs on its leaves. When the ant touches two of these hairs, the leaf snaps shut. Spikes around the edges of the leaves make a cage. The ant gets trapped inside. Surprise! The ant has now become the flytrap's lunch.

The Venus flytrap is no alien from outer space. In fact, it's one of at least 250,000 **species** of plants on earth.

5

INTERVIEW WITH A VENUS FLYTRAP

INTERVIEWER: Mr. Flytrap, people say you're a carnivore, a meat-eating plant.

FLYTRAP: That makes me sound like a bloodthirsty monster. You must be confusing me with some made-up plant in a movie. It's a common mistake. I eat a bug or two now and then. That's all.

INTERVIEWER: Why do you think you are so misunderstood?

FLYTRAP: I think people get a little nervous because I can snap my leaves shut in less than a second. Most people think plants can't move. So when they see me do it, they forget that I'm a plant.

INTERVIEWER: But how do you manage to move?

FLYTRAP: My leaves are spring-loaded like a mousetrap. When a bug lands on one of my leaves, I send a jet of extra water to the leaf. The leaf swells and snaps closed. My meal is trapped.

The Kingdom of Plants

Our planet is crawling with life. There are millions of different living things on Earth. Scientists have not even finished naming all the life forms. To keep track of them all, scientists sort all living things into groups called kingdoms. Plants make up one kingdom. Animals, including people and bugs, make up a separate kingdom.

embryo: the first stage
of growth for a plant

Plants are living things made up of many tiny parts called cells. People and animals are also made of cells. But plant cells look different from animal cells. Plant cells have stiff walls while animal cells have a layer of tissue called a membrane. All plants develop from a small form of the plant called an **embryo**. The embryo is most often found in a seed.

CHAPTER 2

WHAT'S FOR LUNCH?

Like all living things, plants need energy. But hungry plants don't get in a lunch line at school. They get their meals from the sun. What a cool magic trick!

Of course, it's not really magic. It's chemical. You see, plants are green, or at least partly green, for a reason. They have a green substance called **chlorophyll** in some of their cells, usually in their leaves. The chlorophyll collects energy from sunlight. This energy mixes water and minerals from the soil with a gas in the air called carbon dioxide. The plant now has food to survive. This process is known as photosynthesis.

chlorophyll: the green substance in plants that traps sunlight to make food

PHOTOSYNTHESIS

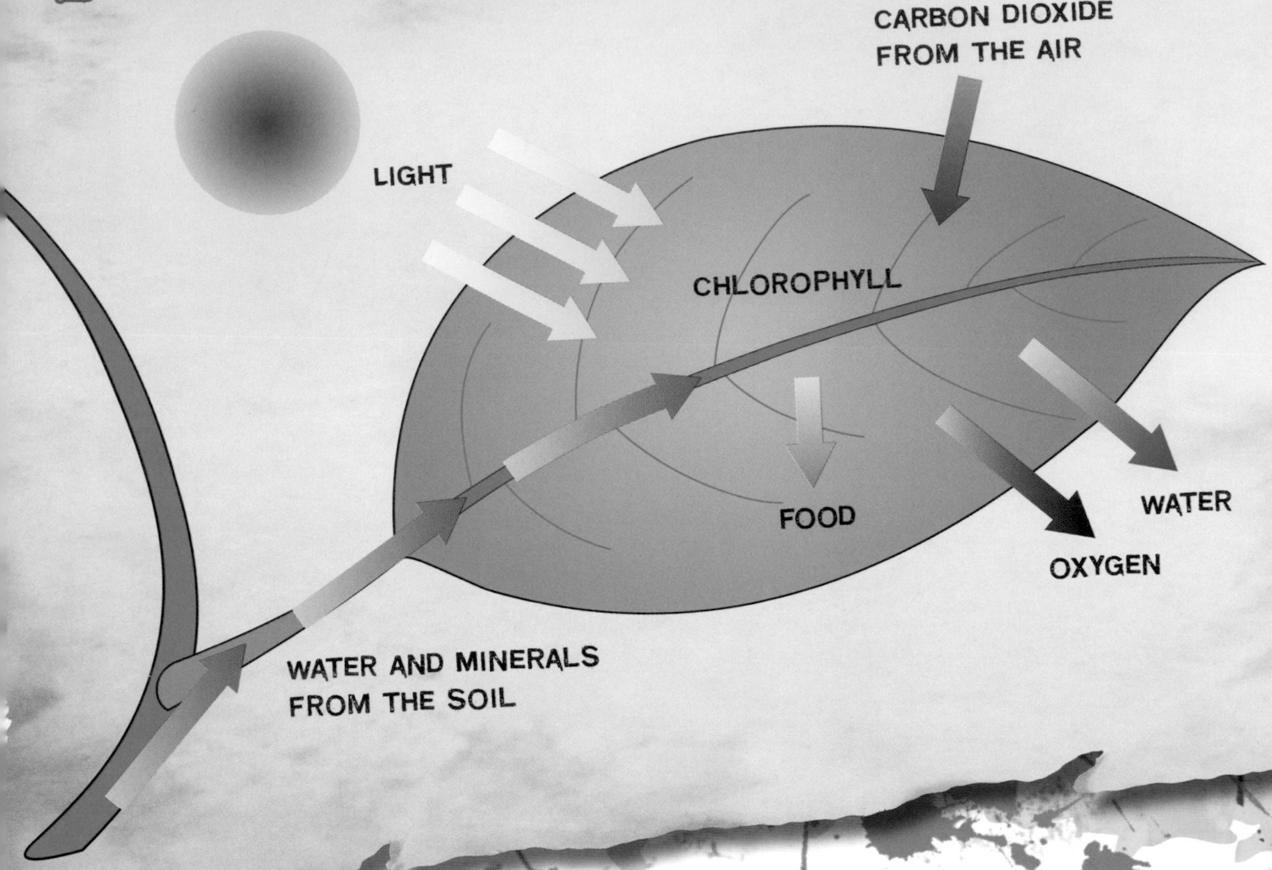

CARBON DIOXIDE
FROM THE AIR

LIGHT

CHLOROPHYLL

FOOD

WATER

OXYGEN

WATER AND MINERALS
FROM THE SOIL

The Truth about Meat-Eating Plants

Most plants are lucky to grow in soil that is rich
in the nutrients needed for photosynthesis. But some
plants grow where the soil doesn't have all of that good
stuff. They do what they can by photosynthesis, but
it's not always enough. To get the nutrients they need,
carnivorous plants add a little meat to their diet.

insectivorous:
depending on insects
for food

But we're not talking about hamburgers and steak. Instead, these plants crave bugs. In fact, some scientists say **insectivorous** is a better way to describe these plants. Some of these plants might super-size their meals with a small frog or lizard now and then. But most of their meat comes from insects.

sundew plant

Slippery Slope and Sticky Situations

Plants can't really stalk their prey. Instead, meat-eating plants trick their prey to get a meal.

Sundew plants are sticky like flypaper. A bug gets stuck on a leaf. The leaf curls inward. Little hairs inside make chemicals that digest the insect.

Pitcher plants collect rainwater. Like many other plants, they make a sweet liquid called nectar. The nectar attracts insects to the plants. When insects land, they slip down into the pitcher and drown. Chemicals in the plants create a bug soup. The plants soak up the nutrient-rich soup through their cell walls.

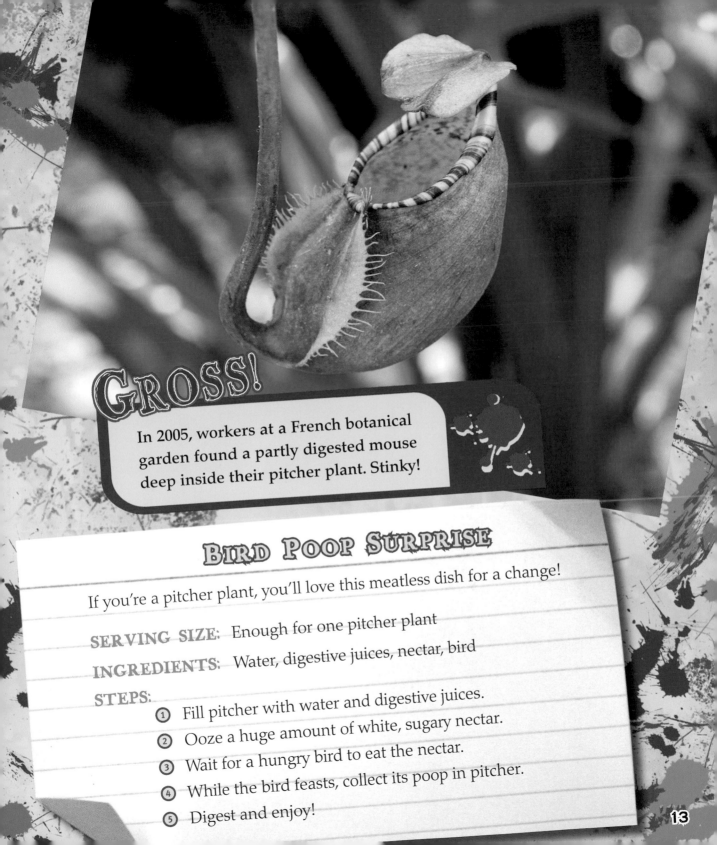

GROSS!

In 2005, workers at a French botanical garden found a partly digested mouse deep inside their pitcher plant. Stinky!

BIRD POOP SURPRISE

If you're a pitcher plant, you'll love this meatless dish for a change!

SERVING SIZE: Enough for one pitcher plant

INGREDIENTS: Water, digestive juices, nectar, bird

STEPS:

1. Fill pitcher with water and digestive juices.
2. Ooze a huge amount of white, sugary nectar.
3. Wait for a hungry bird to eat the nectar.
4. While the bird feasts, collect its poop in pitcher.
5. Digest and enjoy!

13

Bladderworts use trapdoors to catch their prey. They float in quiet ponds or lakes. Trigger hairs cover tiny bubble-like bladders below the surface. The plant sucks the water out of the bladder. When a bug touches a hair, Whoosh! Water and victim rush into the pouch. The bladderwort often takes less than an hour to finish its meal. Then it resets its trap, ready for its next victim.

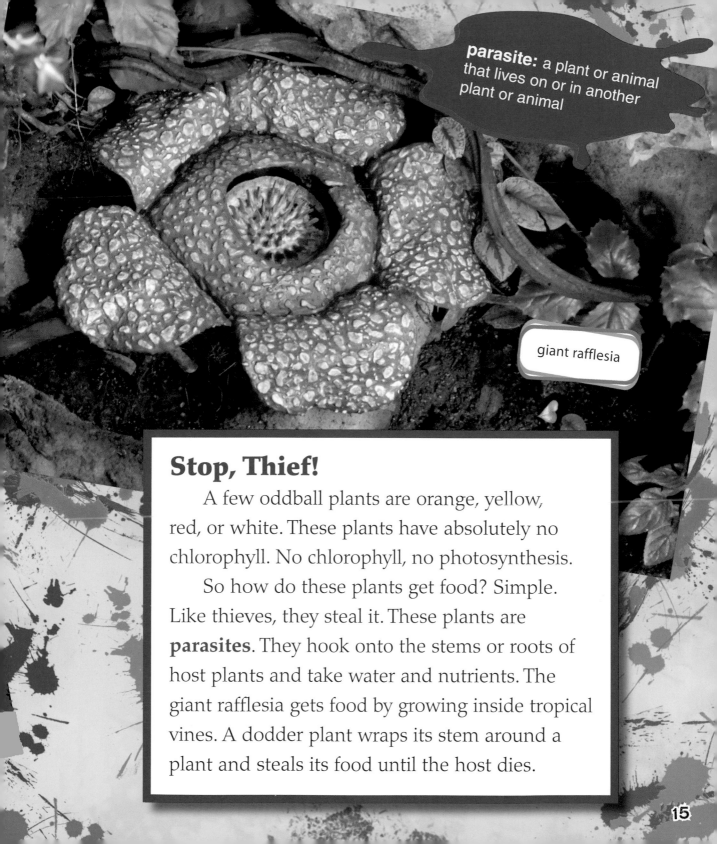

parasite: a plant or animal that lives on or in another plant or animal

giant rafflesia

Stop, Thief!

A few oddball plants are orange, yellow, red, or white. These plants have absolutely no chlorophyll. No chlorophyll, no photosynthesis.

So how do these plants get food? Simple. Like thieves, they steal it. These plants are **parasites**. They hook onto the stems or roots of host plants and take water and nutrients. The giant rafflesia gets food by growing inside tropical vines. A dodder plant wraps its stem around a plant and steals its food until the host dies.

Chapter 3

IT'S NOT EASY BEING A PLANT

From the driest desert to the deepest ocean, plants live in just about every part of the world. To pull it off, plants have adapted some amazing survival skills.

The air on top of Africa's Mount Kenya is cold. When the sun goes down, the air gets even colder. Most plants couldn't survive. But giant groundsel plants hang on. These plants unfold their thick, waxy leaves to soak up daytime sun. At night, the plants fold inward as if to hug themselves. In this way, they stay warm through the night.

CRAZY!

Plants are definitely good at survival. Some scientists believe land plants have been around for 430 million years!

16

Giant groundsel plants take in the sunlight with their large leaves.

If You Can't Take the Heat, Get Out of the Desert

Most plants grow in places where there is some warm weather and plenty of rain. A thirsty plant can't make food. Some plants wither and die in hot, dry weather. So how can a plant live in the desert?

When it comes to water, desert plants have two goals: store more and use less. Desert plants get water out of the air. They hold water for long periods of time in their stems, roots, and leaves. But leaves need a lot of the plant's precious water. So cactuses and some other desert plants don't bother with leaves. They have spines instead.

GROSS!

The Saguaro cactus grows to 66 feet (20 meters) tall. That's as tall as many full-grown oak trees.

The spines on these cactuses protect precious water from hungry and thirsty animals.

wintergreen

Brrr! Some Plants Like It Cold

Not all deserts are hot. The cold air near the north and south poles holds little water. It's dry as a desert. Plants need to make their water last. The leaves of wintergreens have thick, leathery skin. Hairs help hold drops of water too.

Moss plants stay close to the warmth of the ground. Each plant makes a little dome that holds in warm air and water.

acacia tree

Fighting Back

No matter where it grows, no plant wants to become lunch for a hungry animal or bug. But it's not easy for plants to fight off their enemies. Instead, plants have some tricks for staying off the menu.

Acacia trees have ants for bodyguards. Ants live in the trees' hollow thorns. The trees make a sugary food for the ants. In return, the ants attack any other animals that come near the trees.

CHAPTER 4

YOU'VE GOT TO HAVE FRIENDS

Plants and bugs may seem like odd friends. But the plant and animal kingdoms depend on one another to survive.

Some plants use bugs to help make more plants. For example, a titan arum gives off a strong smell like decaying meat. Carrion beetles and sweat bees think they have found a meal. When the bugs don't find any actual dead meat to munch, they move on. But a little bit of the plant's **pollen** sticks to them. If the bugs visit a second titan arum, the pollen transfers to the other plant. Then, a new seed can develop.

pollen: tiny little grains on flowers that help plants make new plants

CRAZY!

The stinky titan arum can grow to be almost 10 feet (3 meters) tall.

TOP 5 AMAZING WAYS PLANTS REPRODUCE

1. Ooze! An herb that grows in China uses slime. A drop of oil containing pollen oozes out of the male part of the flower. The oil spreads to the female part.

2. Hitchhike! The seeds of mountain thistle and some other plants have tiny hooks that stick to the fur of an animal. As the animal wanders, the tag-along seeds fall off and grow into plants.

3. Fly! Hummingbirds and honeybees pick up pollen on their beaks or bodies. They carry the pollen to other flowers as they collect their fill of nectar.

4. Poop! Animals eat fruits or berries, but they often don't digest the seeds. Whole seeds get pooped out along with other body waste. Then the seed begins to grow in a new location. As an extra bonus, the poop provides nutrients for a new plant to grow from the seed.

5. Blast! When touched, the bunchberry dogwood launches pollen with 800 times more force than what an astronaut experiences at blast-off. No other plant, not even the Venus flytrap, can move so fast.

What Goes Around, Comes Around

It's no secret that plants need animals. But people need plants too. Plants give us food. We use the seeds of corn, rice, and wheat plants. Carrots and sweet potatoes are roots. We eat asparagus stems and celery leaves. We eat the flower buds of broccoli and cauliflower.

Without plants, we wouldn't have fruits or vegetables to eat. That might not sound so bad at first. But where else would we get food? Not from meat. The meat we eat comes from animals that eat plants. If plants didn't exist, neither would those animals.

And That's Not All!

It doesn't stop there. During photosynthesis, plants release oxygen into the air. We can't live without oxygen. Many of our medicines come from plants. Wild animals use plants for shelter. Plus, plants hold down soil so it isn't easily swept away by winds or heavy rains.

protea flower

Flower Power!

Plants are all around us. We are so used to seeing trees, flowers, and grasses that we hardly even notice them. But we would notice if they were missing. Weird and wacky plants do a whole lot more than just sit and grow. Plants actually make it possible for other living things, including people, to survive.

TRUE LIVES
OF SCIENTISTS

Some **botanists** think plants would help humans live on Mars. Martian plants would give us more than just fresh food. Plants make oxygen during photosynthesis. They can also get rid of the bad stuff in wastewater, leaving clean water in its place.

Spaced-Out Plants

Botanists study how space conditions affect plants. In 2003, they grew peas on the *International Space Station*. The plants flowered and developed seeds even in the weightless environment of space.

Back on Earth, other botanists are making space-age salads. They planted lettuce in six low-pressure chambers that match the air pressure on Mars. These containers supply the correct amounts of light, heat, and water for plants to grow. Researchers harvest and test the lettuce for quality. They have found that lettuce grows larger than normal in low pressure.

Botanists are developing plants that grow in little or no soil, with less water, or without sunlight. That's good news for future settlers on Mars!

botanist: a scientist who studies plants

29

GLOSSARY

BOTANIST (BAHT-on-ist) — a scientist who studies plants

CHLOROPHYLL (KLOR-uh-fil) — the green substance in plants that uses light to make food from carbon dioxide and water

EMBRYO (EM-bree-oh) — a plant in its first stage of development

INSECTIVOROUS (in-sek-TIV-ur-uhss) — feeding on insects

NUTRIENT (NOO-tree-uhnt) — something that is needed by plants and animals, including people, to stay strong and healthy

PARASITE (PAIR-uh-site) — an animal or plant that needs to live on or inside another animal or plant to survive

PHOTOSYNTHESIS (foh-toh-SIN-thuh-siss) — the process by which green plants make their food

POLLEN (POL-uhn) — tiny grains that flowers produce

SPECIES (SPEE-sheez) — a group of plants or animals that share common characteristics

INTERNET SITES

FactHound offers a safe, fun way to find Internet sites related to this book. All of the sites on FactHound have been researched by our staff.

Here's how:

1. Visit *www.facthound.com*

2. Choose your grade level.

3. Type in this book ID **1429612681** for age-appropriate sites. You may also browse subjects by clicking on letters, or by clicking on pictures and words.

4. Click on the **Fetch It** button.

FactHound will fetch the best sites for you!

READ MORE

Claybourne, Anna. *Plant Secrets: Plant Life Processes.* Fusion. Chicago: Raintree, 2006.

Johnson, Rebecca L. *Carnivorous Plants.* Nature Watch. Minneapolis: Lerner, 2007.

Pike, Katy. *Plants That Bite Back.* The Real Deal. Northborough, Mass.: Chelsea House, 2005.

INDEX